171314 W9-CCO-453

3/98

95-R

C1

B
WARNER   Ellsworth, Mary
              Ellen.

              Gertrude Chandler
              Warner and the
              Boxcar children.

                        30081000051460
$14.95   03/23/1998

C1

B
WARNER   Ellsworth, Mary
              Ellen.

              Gertrude Chandler
              Warner and the
              Boxcar

                        30081000051460
$14.95   03/23/1998

DATE	BORROWER'S NAME	
APR 1 3 1998	3 M	Wendy
26 MAR	Lucy	3M
		4-F

BAKER & TAYLOR